BLACK PATENT LEATHER SHOES

&

TRANSPARENT PIE

*Come with me while I remember the
people I loved and the years that were.
The years were good and
the people even better.*

BLACK PATENT LEATHER SHOES

&

TRANSPARENT PIE

Sydney Burns Turnbull

Mid-Atlantic Highlands

ISBN: 0-9744785-6-3

First Edition
Printed in the U.S.A.

Editorial Coordination: John Patrick Grace
  and Jennifer Adkins
Cover Painting: Dr. William Grimes
Interior Design: Jennifer Adkins

Mid-Atlantic Highlands
An imprint of Publishers Place, Inc.
945 Fourth Avenue, Suite 200A
Huntington, WV 25701
www.publishersplace.org

This book was begun in the Life Writing Class at the Huntington Museum of Art with John Patrick Grace, Ph.D., in January 2003.

Dedicated to the memory of my husband,
William C. Turnbull,
who always told me, "You should write."

ACKNOWLEDGEMENTS

My appreciation to Dr. William L. Grimes, who painted the lovely picture of my home in Louisa, Kentucky for the front cover.

My appreciation to Mr. Greg Goodall, the printer who made the cover come alive and helped me with the design of the book.

My appreciation to Dr. John Patrick Grace, who helped me through all the phases of writing this book and kept encouraging me all along the way.

I.

THESE ARE THE YEARS THAT WERE

This is the place stand still my steed
Let me view the scene
And summon from the shadowy past
The forms that once have been.
—Longfellow

The last guest had left, and I was alone on the balcony looking out at the stars and the lights below and listening to the crickets and the tree frogs—the sounds of summer—the sounds transported me back to another summer and another place.

It was a hot and humid summer day when I met my friend Margaret for the first time; I was eight and she was ten. She and her parents had moved back to her mother's home, and I met them at church on Sunday.

"Home" was a very picturesque little town in eastern Kentucky named Louisa. It lay in the Big Sandy Valley between the hills of eastern Kentucky and the Big Sandy River. It was a town with quiet, peaceful streets shaded by oaks and elms and maples and where most of the families went back for generations. Life was never hurried, and people always had time to stop and visit. Everyone I knew went to church on Sunday; the older ladies in their lace dresses and antique jewelry strolled sedately down the street, the teenage girls in their first "high heels" wobbled down the street, and then there was me. I and all my friends wore black patent leather shoes and white socks—and I hated 'em!

Louisa was founded in 1822, and its newspaper, *The Big Sandy News*, was the oldest paper in the valley. By comparison, the state of West Virginia wasn't formed until 1863, making Louisa forty-one years older than West Virginia. The Methodist church was the first church established in Louisa and was the only church for such a long time that the fiscal court of the county, under authority gained through a special act of the legislature, granted it a site on the corner of the courthouse square.

The church erected its first building some years before the Civil War. During the Civil War the church was badly abused by the Union soldiers, who used it to quarter their horses. This is the church that my family had attended for generations and the church where I met Margaret that hot summer Sunday.

Louisa was a friendly town, clean and pretty. It was home to two Methodist churches (one Northern, one Southern), the Southern Methodist being the one located on the courthouse square; two Baptist churches and one Christian church. I had attended vacation Bible School at most of them.

The town had a picture show, two private tennis courts, one public one, and lots of yards full of croquet players. It was the county seat of Lawrence County and had a beautiful old red brick courthouse with a sign over the entrance asking "Reader, Where Wilt Thou Spend Eternity?" A picture of the courthouse with the entrance sign was featured in *Life* magazine, along with a picture and article about Fred M. Vinson, the 13th Chief Justice of the United States, who had been born and reared in Louisa.

The Southern Methodist church was on one side of the courthouse, but on the other side was a large white gazebo where people from all over the county came together on Saturdays to visit. Sometimes sweet music could be heard drifting across the grass. It was fun to get an ice cream cone from the drug store across the street and then go and stand in the courthouse yard to listen to the "fiddle" players, guitar strummers and accordion players.

Our high school building was interesting as well as architecturally attractive. It had a bell tower atop a three-story red brick building—when the bell rang you had three minutes to get to your classroom. It had formerly been "Kentucky Normal College," presided over by Professor Byington. Due to political pressure the college was moved to Morehead, Kentucky, and became Morehead State College.

Our grade school sat at the foot of the town hill, and the teachers had a hard time keeping the boys off the hill during recess. The last two years I went to the grade school I rode my bicycle with several friends. I lived only six blocks from school, but bicycling was much more fun than walking.

We had only one "avenue" in town; the rest were "streets." Our one avenue, which started beside my house, was named "Lock Avenue" because it went north to the Lock and Needle Dam about twelve blocks away. It was almost perfectly straight and a wonderful place to ride bicycles. The dam was the first lock and needle dam in the United States and was quite a distance below the street, not easily seen unless you got off your bicycle and walked to the edge of the high bank. Louisa sat on very high ground.

Right in the middle of town on the street

behind the courthouse was a two-lane cobble-stone street leading down to the river. It had once been used for loading and unloading mate-rials that came by boat to eastern Kentucky, but now only the showboats stopped there once or twice during the summer. They were lots of fun, and people came from everywhere to see the shows. The calliope could be heard for several miles before the boat arrived, and we all rushed to the river to watch it come in to dock. It was exciting to walk across the wooden plank, over the water, to the boat. The show had a full house every night.

Once when I was riding with Mother, she rode her horse, "Colonel," down the cobblestone street to the river so he could get a drink of water. Colonel was named, sort of, by me. When I was five years old I was commissioned a Kentucky Colonel by Governor Sampson. I was only the second girl to be so honored. The first girl to be commissioned was Shirley Temple.

The town had two hospitals and several doctors, but if you needed surgery a surgeon from out of town would be called in. One hospital, Louisa General, was on Lock Avenue not far from my house, and the other, Riverview, was closer to the middle of town on the street adjacent to the Southern Methodist Church and, as its name suggests, on the bank of the river.

The town was cut in half by the C & O Railroad. We had four passenger trains a day, two in the morning, and two in the afternoon. By taking these trains to larger cities like Cincinnati, Ohio, you could get connections to anywhere in the country. We went to Cincinnati several times a year.

Fortunately my family lived on the same side of town as the fire department. We had a wonderful volunteer fire department and a shiny red fire engine. All my family lived on this side of the railroad and Margaret's did, too, so we didn't need to worry about the fire engine getting to us if there were a train blocking the track.

Our families had been friends for several generations. In 1847 Margaret's great-great grandfather, Congressman Laben T. Moore, gave to my great-great uncle, Rowland T. Burns, who was a lawyer, a Spanish or bald cypress tree and planted it on the front lawn of great-great Uncle Rowland's house. Congressman Moore had obtained it from the Botanical Gardens in Washington, D. C. It was said that it was the only tree of this particular species in the state and only the second in the entire United States. The Burns boys referred to it as the "Courtin' Tree."

The tree measured five feet in diameter and one hundred feet high, and it had one hundred limbs. Its leaves were deciduous. In summer they were green and in autumn they turned red and brown. The cones were tubular and appeared irregularly along the branches. They dropped from the tree, burst open upon striking the ground and were very fragrant, being filled with rich oil. However, this cone-bearing tree, which is not an evergreen, does not produce cones every year.

Bald (Spanish) cypress tree in Uncle Rowland's yard.

Louisa's history went from the famous to the infamous. Louisa could boast of Fred M. Vinson, 13th Chief Justice of the United States, whose sons Freddie and Jim Bob were great friends of mine. Freddie, who was only a few years older than I, gave me the dress I was christened in.

On the infamous side, it was rumored that Jesse James was buried in Lawrence County. Shortly after the Huntington National Bank in Huntington, West Virginia was robbed by the "James Gang," a lone cowboy came riding into Lawrence County. He rode onto a farm located in the southern end of the county. He got a job on this farm and said that his name was Jack Johnson. This seemed plausible since the initials on his saddle bags were "J.J."

After a couple of years on the farm Jack Johnson moved into Louisa and opened a livery stable. He also had a funeral carriage with horses for rent. When Jack Johnson died no family members were ever located. He is buried somewhere in Lawrence County. We may never know the true identity of the man who called himself "Jack Johnson."

NEWS FLASH !!

In the late 1990s a body, presumed for years to be that of Jesse James and interred in Missouri, was exhumed for a positive identification. The DNA from the body and that taken from the descendants of Jesse James proved once and for all that the body was NOT that of Jesse James!

So...

II.

A LITTLE OF MY HISTORY

Margaret was a pretty girl with naturally curly brown hair, brown eyes and fair skin. She was a little taller than I since she was older. I, on the other hand, had blue eyes and light brown hair and was always thin, so people were forever trying to "fatten me up." I made the Honor Roll every month at school and I was sure Margaret would, too. We lived in similar houses a block apart. The houses were spacious with large yards. Our grandparents had lived in these houses, and my grandfather still did.

Margaret's yard was enclosed by a not-so-high hedge, and mine, because of our dogs, was surrounded by an iron fence. Only one of our dogs ever jumped the fence—a German shepherd named Mark, who used to jump it at will like a deer. Our Airedales used to try it too as they watched Mark vault over. They would run at the fence and then have to stop short. Airedales aren't made to jump. Then they would stand there and bark loudly at Mark, who was now on the other side.

My grandfather loved fruit trees and my grandmother loved flowers, so our yard was full of both. My grandmother had tulips, peonies, hydrangea, iris, a rose arbor over the back walk, and three magnolias as tall as our three-story house. She also grew gardenias; she had twenty pots that in summer sat outside, but that in winter were put into "The Pit" in the back yard.

The "Pit" was six feet deep and twelve feet long by five feet wide with cement sides and a dirt floor. There was a ladder inside so we could reach the flowers. All this was covered by a removable top of glass panes in a wooden frame. I was not allowed near the "Pit," but in summer my job was to water the gardenias every evening. There were also red begonias in pots that sat on top of the railing that surrounded the front porch. I watered these too.

My grandfather, not to be outdone, had planted a cherry tree, a peach tree, a crab apple tree and two Golden Delicious apple trees. The yard also had a large oak tree that held my swing from one of its branches. There was barely enough room left for my croquet set! My grandmother had died when I was six, but my mother had kept all her flowers the way they had always been.

It was summer, so I was outside in the yard a lot. I had fun playing with my dog, Sandy, and my ten outside cats (more or less!). The cats were always having kittens and one of my favorites, who was black and white and named "Snowball," was expecting a litter soon. I had fixed up a cat hospital from a crate turned sideways with an old rug hung over the opening and towels on the floor. I thought Margaret might like to see it, so I walked over to her house. There she was, perched up in an apple tree eating an apple.

She waved and said, "Hi, come on up." So I climbed the tree and sat down beside her. "Grab an apple," she said. I reached out and got one. She started to take a bite of hers when I saw a worm in it. "Don't eat that!" I screamed. "There's a worm in it!"

She looked down her nose at me and said, "I like worms" and bit into the apple anyway. She ate half a worm! She took another bite and got the other half! I was stunned but impressed. I had never known anyone who ate worms. I almost forgot why I came, and then I remembered Snowball.

I told Margaret about the "hospital" and

asked if she would like to see it. She said she would. So we climbed down the apple tree, told her mother and went back to my house. We went in the back gate since the cats were all in the back. I took her to the crate and lifted up the rug so she could see the "hospital," and lo and behold, there was Snowball with five black and white babies, all blind with little cords attached to their little stomachs.

I called Mother to come quick and see. She couldn't believe that Snowball had actually had her kittens where she was supposed to. Then we got all kinds of orders: "Don't touch, don't raise the carpet and let the light in, and don't bring all your friends to see them." Supposedly if we did any of these things Snowball would move them where we couldn't find them. In ten days their eyes would open and the cords would drop off their little stomachs, and maybe we could touch them. We did as we were told, except I peeked at them once a day.

In a month the kittens were wobbling around and playing. Sandy snoozed on the back porch a lot in summer, and the kittens decided he was a wonderful mountain to climb, so they climbed all over him, and from time to time their little claws got caught in his hair and stuck him. He would raise his head and stare at them, and if they didn't get the message he would get up and shake slowly and gently until they fell off.

If they came back he would gently pick up each kitten in his mouth and take it to the far end of the yard; when he got them all taken care of he could nap in peace, since it took them an hour to find their way back. Snowball never minded. She and Sandy were old friends. My grandfather did, though; he said we couldn't have kittens meowing all over the yard. He loved his horses and the dogs but didn't think much of cats. After all, cats killed birds and he loved birds. He had a special canary that came from Omaha and was a wonderful singer.

My parents had divorced when I was a baby, and Mother and I had always lived with my grandparents. My grandfather was the "father" in my life, and I adored him. I called him "Daddy" because Mother did. I was beyond happy living with my grandparents and Mother. I was named for my grandfather, Milton Sidney Burns, who was a wise and altogether delightful man. He loved and was loved by the children—he carried candy in his pocket for them—and was greatly respected by the adults. He was both a doctor and a lawyer, as well as a story teller extraordinaire. He could hypnotize me by sitting in his chair and peeling an entire apple while I watched the peel spiral to the floor without ever breaking.

I would sit spellbound on the floor beside

his chair and listen to his stories, which always began with "Once upon a time, when this country was nothing but a howling wilderness inhabited by only wild Indians and bears and wolves..." At which point he would howl softly like a wolf, and when you were properly scared with the hair standing up on the back of your neck, he would begin his story.

He had a cast of characters that remained the same in all his stories: Ring, the faithful dog; Willie, the small bear; and Cupid the pony. They accompanied my grandfather in all his stories. He would put me in his stories riding Cupid with Ring and Willie running along beside us. We were scouts for the Army looking for Indians on the town hill. To hear my grandfather's stories, we had found lots of Indians for the Army!

He had graduated from the University of Cincinnati Medical College because his mother had wanted him to be a doctor. However, he couldn't stand the sight of blood, so he became a lawyer instead and later a judge.

He had been born in Prestonsburg, Kentucky, and had a horrendous and exciting experience when he was just a child. During the Civil War, Colonel James A. Garfield, who commanded the Union troops who occupied Prestonsburg, made his headquarters in the Burns' home. The stately, white-painted house was only nine years old when Colonel Garfield commandeered it in 1862. My great-grandfather was in Mt. Sterling, Kentucky, on a business trip.

The night the colonel moved in he found my great-grandmother, Kizzie Clay Burns (for whom my mother was named), who was critically ill; my grandfather, Milton S. Burns, who was only six years old; and his brother, Rowland, who was sixteen years old. The Union troops came looting into Prestonsburg, and a group of the soldiers barged into great-grandfather's house and "appropriated" great-grandmother's gold watch and $17 before Garfield arrived.

That night Rowland, my grandfather Milton, and another youth, working in silence, carried my great-grandmother on her mattress down to the river bank, placed her on a flat boat and pushed off from shore. The boys poled the boat all the way downstream to Louisa, taking advantage of the current.

Colonel Garfield stayed in this home for ten days and became so enamored of it that he bought it after the war. But after he became President of the United States, he never returned to live in it.

There was a very small town across the Big Sandy river from Louisa named Fort Gay, West Virginia. The only way to reach it was by ferry boat. My grandfather thought a bridge was needed across the river so the towns could trade with each other more easily. Thus he founded "The Louisa-Fort Gay Bridge Company" and began to sell stock in the company to pay for building the bridge. It was to be a toll bridge, which would also help pay expenses. He rode horseback all over the county selling the stock. He promised the buyers that they would not lose their money, but they probably wouldn't make any money. The people trusted him and in no time there was enough money to build the bridge.

The bridge opened around 1902-1903 to lots of fanfare; it helped the area more than anything else had ever done. It appeared in Ripley's "Believe It or Not" column as the only bridge in the world to join two states, two townships, two counties, cross two bodies of water, and cross three pieces of land. The third piece of land was between the Tug Fork and the Levisa Fork; at Louisa they joined to form the Big Sandy River.

The piece of land between the Tug Fork and the Levisa Fork was known as "The Point Section," and there were lots of homes there. It was great fun when visitors came to town looking for a residence on the "Point," to tell them to go to the middle of the bridge and turn right!

Bridge across the Big Sandy River joining Louisa, Kentucky and Fort Gay, West Virginia.

My grandfather was also a devoted fan of the Louisa Bulldogs football team. When they had a winning season he always had a banquet for the team and the coach. He was a pillar in the Southern Methodist Church and president of the First National Bank of Louisa. He rode his horse, "Lasses" (short for Molasses because she was the color of Molasses), up in the hills around Louisa almost every day and took Sandy with him. Her pedigreed name was Lady Margaret J., and he was so attached to her that he had a sculpture made of her.

Mother sometimes rode with my grandfather in the hills. She once rode to school at recess and took me for a short ride on the hill behind the school. I just crawled out the classroom window right on to the horse's back and we rode off. This was done with the teacher's permission, of course. I had to be very careful of the pencil sharpener, which was on the window ledge, as I crawled out the window.

III.

MORE FAMILY

My great-Aunt Lillian Reynolds and her daughter, Louise Milton Reynolds, lived on the street parallel to Margaret's. Aunt Lill's garage backed up to Margaret's barn. My great aunt was the much younger sister of my grandmother. Her husband had been a doctor and died during the big flu epidemic of 1911-1912. I loved visiting with her. She always treated me like an adult and told wonderful stories. She also allowed me to drink Coca-Cola, which they didn't at home. I spent many happy hours on her porch or in her den, talking with her as if I were her age or she were mine. Like the rest of us, she had an Airedale. His name was "Noisey," and he did bark a lot.

My cousin, Louise Milton, was most attractive and had lots of dates. She had black hair, which she wore pulled back from her face in a bun at the nape of her neck. She had wonderful bone structure and looked beautiful with her hair that way. Occasionally she took me along on her dates. Once she and her date took me to the circus. Her date bought all sorts of peanuts, popcorn and candy for me until Louise M. stopped him. She said I would surely get sick. I didn't, but he did!

She took me ice skating on the river with her friends. One time we skated at night. The lockmaster turned the lights on over the dam and we skated there. We built a fire on the river bank so we could get warm when we got too cold skating. That was lots of fun, even more fun than skating in the daytime. Bernard Wells, one of the older men in town who liked to skate, always checked the thickness of the ice before we could skate. In fact, he checked it early in the day, so we could plan on skating in the after-noon or at night.

Aunt Lill had a cleaning woman named Mrs. Moore who was very jealous of her husband, and everyone seemed to know about it. One day after her husband had finished his lunch, which she packed for him every day, his friends slipped a note into his lunch box and signed a woman's name. Mrs. Moore found the note, of course, but she didn't question him about it.

After supper she asked him to climb up on the roof and look for a leak she thought they had. He went in the garage and got the ladder, propped it against the house, and climbed up on the roof. As soon as he was on the roof, Mrs. Moore took the ladder away and picked up her shotgun. She proceeded to shoot him off the roof and then went inside and called the funeral home. When the hearse arrived they couldn't find "the body"! Fortunately for him, while she was a good cleaner, she was a poor shot. Needless to say, she didn't work for my great-aunt after that.

IV.

THE TEA PARTY

I had just finished watering the flowers when Margaret came walking through our front gate. "I'm all finished so I can play now," I called.

"I've come to invite you to a tea party," Margaret answered, "But I can't play now, I have to deliver the other invitations." The party was to be on Saturday afternoon at her house. I couldn't wait to tell Mother. I loved parties, but until now I'd only been to birthday parties. Mother could tell me all about tea parties, and Margaret and I had had pretend tea parties, but never a real one.

I found Mother playing the piano, as usual; that was her favorite thing to do. I always enjoyed listening to her and she could play anything I wanted, but today I was excited about the tea party. "Mother," I cried, "I've been invited to a tea party!"

"Where?" said Mother.

"At Margaret's house on Saturday," I answered.

"How nice! You'll get to wear your party dress."

"And," I ventured, "my black patent leather shoes? Ugh!"

"Well, they are your good shoes."

I called my Aunt Shirley, Mother's sister, to tell her about the party. She and Margaret's aunt were old friends, and she had been to many parties in that house when she was young. She liked parties, too, so she wanted to know all about the tea party.

Finally Saturday came and I got dressed for the party. I wore my pretty pink dress with a pink sash, and Mother put two pink bows in my hair. She had parted my hair in the middle with a pink bow on each side. I had asked her to roll my hair last night, so today I had curls. Since I only had a block to walk, my clothes were still in good shape when I got there.

Margaret answered the door wearing her party dress, and we went into the library to wait for the other girls. Once everyone was there Margaret's mother, Mrs. Codding, wheeled in a tea cart holding hot chocolate, cookies and tiny cheese balls with red coloring and a small leaf stuck in each one so that they looked like little apples. She served the hot chocolate in antique demitasse cups with a large spoonful of whipped cream on the top. Oooooh! that was good—so good that I had four cups! The tea party was as much fun as I had thought it would be. We all had a wonderful time.

When I got home I told Mother all about the party and what a good time I had. I told her about the hot chocolate with the whipped cream and that it was so good I had four cups. She said, "You had what?"

"I had four cups, it was delicious." She was "undone"—it seemed that young ladies didn't have four cups of anything! She said that I probably wouldn't be invited for hot chocolate again anytime soon. I saw Margaret and her parents at church on Sunday and they treated me just the same, so I hoped Mother was wrong.

Mother was a pretty lady with brown hair and big brown eyes. She was slender, not too tall and wore such pretty clothes—I thought she was just about perfect. She was the most "lady-like" woman I knew and also the most fun. She knew all about how young ladies should behave. She played the piano really well and the violin, too. She had graduated from the Cincinnati Conservatory of Music and often played the violin at church as well as for special occasions. I have never heard "Panis Angelicus" played more beautifully than when mother played it.

She was the choir director at our church and started a junior choir for young people aged eight to fifteen. Margaret and I were both in the choir. There were boys and girls in the choir, but more girls. We held bake sales and candy sales to help pay for our white choir robes. We sang on Sunday evenings, and there were almost as many people on Sunday evenings as on Sunday morning—they enjoyed the junior choir.

The church had two aisles, so we divided and marched down both aisles and up three steps to the choir loft behind the pulpit. We always sang a favorite hymn as we marched in, and the congregation loved it. We had lots of fun singing in the choir; Mother had parties at home for us and in summer took us on picnics.

I enjoyed reading a lot, so Mother would let me read in bed with her on the weekends. She ordered *Wee Wisdom* for me to read while she read her *Ladies Home Journal*. I felt so grown-up and had such fun. I got to stay up until ten o'clock on Friday and Saturday, reading in bed. I loved reading books, too; my favorites were the Lassie books, as well as books about Black Beauty, the Bobbsey Twins, the Little Colonel, and Nancy Drew. I couldn't remember a time when I didn't like to read. Mother said she taught me to read before I went to school, in self-defense, because she got tired of reading the Sunday funny paper to me over and over!

V.

MATTIE

Mattie was our housekeeper. She had a great sense of humor and was fun to be around. In the evenings, after supper, she and I would go for a walk and get cones at the ice cream parlor and sometimes we would go to the picture show. We played cards a lot too. I had played cards for so long that I didn't remember when I had learned.

Mattie was as strict with me as Mother was. There were some children she didn't want me to play with or have come to the house. When I asked her why she just said, "They're some-timey."

I asked, "What is sometimey?"

She answered, "Sometimes they speak and sometimes they don't, and they never make good friends." Well, I certainly looked out for "sometimey" people after that.

She didn't think much of our church dinners, either. When Mother would tell her that she didn't have to cook because we were going to the church dinner, she would just shake her head. Finally, one day I asked her why she shook her head, "Because you get those 'see-more' dinners at church," she answered. I was puzzled, I had never heard of "see-more" dinners, so I asked her what they were. She explained that at church dinners you "see more of the plate than you do the dinner." I'd have to pay close attention from now on.

She was so good to my grandfather that it made us love her all the more, and her Transparent Pie was just the best ever. Transparent Pie was "born and raised" in Eastern Kentucky, and the recipe was well over a hundred years old. Mattie used my grandmother's recipe.

Mattie also had dates. There were several nice men in Louisa that she dated, but one of her dates, "James," was particularly interesting. He was from Huntington, West Virginia, and was the chauffeur for Mr. James D. Francis. Mr. Francis was the president of Island Creek Coal Company. My friends and I always got a good laugh when we saw this long black car parked at my back gate when James came calling on

Mattie!

One night, though, James hadn't brought Mattie home by one o'clock, and Mother was very upset. She called Mr. Francis and proceeded to tell him what a lovely young woman Mattie was and that she had never stayed out this late before and she was worried sick. Mr. Francis assured Mother that James was very trustworthy and that the couple would be home soon. He was sure that James had not had an accident or he would have been called. Mattie did get home within the next hour, and Mother was waiting up for her, ready to call Mr. Francis again if need be. I'm sure that if James had been the chauffeur for the President of the United States, Mother would have called him, too.

TRANSPARENT PIE

1/2 cup butter
1 cup sugar
4 eggs, separated
2 tablespoons cornstarch mixed in 1/2 cup milk
1 teaspoon vanilla
pinch of salt

Cream butter and 1/2 cup sugar. Beat egg yolks and rest of sugar. Add vanilla and cornstarch/milk. Add all to butter and sugar mixture and mix well. Pour into slightly baked pie shell. Bake at 350 degrees for 40 minutes. While baking stir down with a fork several times until done.

Meringue:
Beat egg whites until fluffy and big, then add 2 tablespoons of sugar per egg white, beating well after each addition. Add a little vanilla. Spoon on top of pie and bake at 400 degrees for 10 minutes or until lightly browned.

VI.

THE ENTREPRENEURS

It was the middle of summer, and we wanted to do something different. I thought maybe we could make gardenia perfume and sell it. I had enough gardenias at my house for us to do this. We could boil the petals, and that would surely make perfume. Margaret thought that we might use other flower petals, too, like roses and lilies. It all sounded good, so we got to work on it.

We collected the gardenia petals and the rose petals at my house and the lily petals at Margaret's. We boiled them at my house on the back porch, where we had a stove that Mattie used in summer to keep the house cool. We also had a summer kitchen attached to the back porch, where Sarah Jones did the washing and ironing. Sarah was just about the sweetest woman you could ever know.

We boiled the petals awhile until we thought the water smelled good, and then we took the pan off the stove to cool. The trouble was that it looked like water, not perfume. We went to the ten-cent store to see what we could find to color the water. We found a bottle of red liquid; the label said "Brilliantine," but we didn't know what that was, and it was such a pretty color that we bought it.

We added it to our "flower water" perfume, and our perfume turned pink. Next we had to find some small bottles to put it in. We finally found ten small bottles, filled them up, and were ready to start selling. We thought that grown-ups would be more likely to buy perfume than our friends, so we started with them first.

We called on several of our parents' friends, but found no one at home until we called at Mrs. Snyder's house. (Mrs. Snyder's grandson, Gus, was in my class at school.) She didn't answer the door, so we went around back. We knocked on the door and Bessie Reed opened it. She was a friend of Mattie's and was the housekeeper for the Snyders. I knew her well and liked her a lot. She asked, "What are you girls doing?"

We showed her a bottle and said, "We're selling perfume for a nickel a bottle. Would you like one?" Her boyfriend was sitting in the kitchen with her, so she told him to buy a bottle for her. He gave us the nickel and we gave her the perfume. Our first sale! What fun!

We continued down the street, where we ran into several of our friends. We told them what we were doing and asked if they wanted to buy a bottle.

One friend, Patsy, said she wanted one, so we sold her our second bottle. She was dabbing it on her neck when some got on the collar of her dress and stained it! She got mad and said, "I want my nickel back!" We gave her her nickel back and decided that the perfume business might get us into trouble, so we quit right then and there.

Several days later we were still in a "business mood," so we wondered if maybe we could make soap and sell it. We bought some powdered soap and a lot of paper cups that were used to hold hot liquids. We boiled the powder in water, and when it began to get thick we took it off the stove. After it cooled we poured it into the cups and put the lids on the cups.

It had turned a pretty shade of green, so we named it "Jade Magic Soap." We decided to advertise. We went to the newspaper office and bought some white cardboard and cut it into four strips. Margaret could draw real pretty, so she drew the pictures and I made up the slogans. On two strips she drew a beautiful girl and I wrote "New York Deb prefers Jade Magic Soap." On the other two strips she drew a little boy who had just spilled ink on the carpet, so I wrote, "Quick, the Jade Magic!" We nailed these to the telephone poles on Main Street.

Now once more we were ready for business, and again we were going to go door to door. Margaret found an old satchel that had belonged to her grandfather. Mother thought this was too funny because the handle, which was in the middle of the satchel, fell to the bottom of the satchel when you let it go. We didn't mind, though, because it held all of our "stuff." We had a bottle of water, some Jade Magic Soap and some rags. This was so we could demonstrate. And of course, we had some soap to sell.

We went first to our Sunday school teacher's house, which was newly built and beautiful. We rang the doorbell, and when she came to the door we told her about our soap and offered to demonstrate it on her new white front door. She said, "No, no, you don't need to demonstrate; I'll buy some." That was easy! We sold a lot of soap that way. People said they didn't need a demonstration; they just bought the soap. Within two days we had sold all our soap.

Now we were ready to do something else. We'd already sold perfume and soap, so we couldn't do that again. What else could we do? We thought and thought while we were lying in the grass at Margaret's, looking up at the blue sky and the white billowy clouds. The clouds always seemed to take on forms—one minute a rabbit and the next a cat. It was such a lazy summer day. We couldn't think forever, though; as soon as the whistle on the four-thirty train sounded, I had to go home. The train was everyone's signal to go home. It was time to take a bath and get dressed for supper.

We finally got an idea: we could have a play! We could have it in Margaret's barn loft, since mine was full of hay for the horses and old *National Geographics*. What would we do about furniture, a curtain and seats for our audience? We would have to figure those out. The train whistle blew and I had to go home, but I waited until the train pulled into the station. As I left, Margaret called, "Come back after supper and we'll work on the play some more." I waved and nodded.

After supper I went back to Margaret's to talk about the play. We decided we could put up a rope from one side of the loft to the other and hang blankets over it for curtains. We needed some furniture, and we found an old fireplace mantel in the loft that we could use in the middle of the stage. Then we found an old spinning wheel and finally an old straw rug. That was as much furniture as we could find, so we decided that was enough.

What could we use for seats for our audience? We looked around and found a stack of lumber; we could use some planks if we could find something to put them on. We looked out the loft door—which was one floor from the ground—and spotted a pile of bricks in the back yard. The sidewalk around Margaret's house was brick, and her parents were having the bricks taken up and a cement walk put down. Those bricks would be perfect! We could pile them up on either side of the loft and put the wooden planks on top. We could make several rows this way.

We decided the play would be a ghost story. I wanted to be the ghost, and Margaret took the part of the heroine. Next we had to get our friends to play the other parts. We asked three girls and they thought it would be lots of fun. We had our first practice and decided what each of us would wear. My costume was the easiest; all I needed was a white sheet.

We thought we should charge five cents a ticket, but we had to print the tickets some way. We bought construction paper at the ten-cent Store and cut it into strips and wrote "five cents" on each strip. We got the tickets made and began selling them. We did really well—we sold out!

The time came for our last rehearsal. Everything was going well, except my mother wouldn't let me have a sheet and cut eye holes in it. I didn't know what I was going to do! One of the girls spoke up and said she had just the thing, she had found it in her grandmother's trunk. I was sooooo glad to hear that. I told her to bring it tomorrow.

The day had arrived for the play; we all gathered in the loft and put on our costumes. Our audience began to arrive, climbing the stairs to the loft, which were just like the stairs in the house except really dirty.

When everyone got seated the play began. There were a few scenes before the ghost appeared, then it was time for me. I came from behind the mantel, waving my arms up and down and moaning, "Oooo," when all of a sudden a collective gasp swept around the room!

I had thought my costume was perfect. It was a lot like our junior choir robes, except it had a hood with eyeholes. The only problem was the big, black initials on the front—KKK!

The play closed early. My mother was horrified and wanted to know where I had gotten such a costume. She said that NONE of our family had ever belonged to the KKK. You see, none of our families had ever told us about the

Ku Klux Klan, so we knew nothing about it. Doesn't this speak well for my little southern town?

Margaret Codding (left) and Sydney Burns Lindsey

VII.

BICYCLING

Margaret already had a bicycle when she moved to Louisa—a blue Hawthorne—and she rode it a lot. I had skates but no bicycle— yet. Mother had driven to Ashland the week before to look at bicycles. I found one that I really liked, a bright red Elgin, so mother bought it and the store was shipping it to Louisa (which meant that it was coming on the 4:30 train). I wanted a basket on it so I could carry my books, since I planned on riding it to school every day. The new bicycle was due tomorrow, and I could hardly wait! I didn't know how to ride, but I was sure I could learn quickly.

Mother, Daddy, Aunt Shirley and Margaret all went to the station with me to get my bicycle. It came on the 4:30 p.m. train from

Ashland, Kentucky. It was just beautiful! And I was so glad I had picked a red one!

They uncrated it at the station, and Daddy held it for me to get on. It had looked so easy when everyone else rode bicycles, but it wasn't! I couldn't even make the pedals go around one time before it turned over and I had to jump off! This was no fun at all. Since we couldn't put the bicycle in the car and take it home, Mother asked Margaret to ride it home. That made me just a tad mad! Margaret got to ride my new bicycle before I did. Nothing about getting my new bicycle seemed fair.

The next morning when I woke up, Mother said to hurry and dress and come to breakfast. After breakfast Mother wheeled my bicycle out into the yard and said, "Now, we're going to practice riding your bicycle. You can't hurt it if it falls on the ground, but you could knock the paint off if it falls on the sidewalk." So, once more I climbed on my new bicycle. Mother held it by the back of the seat so it couldn't turn over.

"Now, pedal," she said.

I did, and as long as she held on I could stay on.

"You must learn to balance," she told me.

But that I felt was impossible. Every time she let go, the bicycle wobbled and turned over.

"There's a certain feeling to balancing, and

you have to find that feeling of balance. It just takes a little time," my mother soothed.

We practiced all day, only stopping for lunch, and by supper time I could ride a little way around the yard. It was beginning to be fun. The next day I practiced in the yard again, but by afternoon I took to the sidewalk.

At last I could ride a bicycle! I was careful, but I could now "feel" the balance that Mother had talked about. I could go riding with my friends and run all sorts of errands for Mother. I just wanted to ride all the time! I still liked skating, but you could go faster on a bicycle. My friends Mary Jane, Margaret and Beth Ann and I could spend most of the afternoons riding all over town. None of us minded running errands for our mothers, since we could ride our bicycles and a lot of the time go together.

Margaret and I had just come back from riding to the lower end of town to get fresh buttermilk for supper. My family all liked buttermilk, but I thought it tasted terrible! After we took the buttermilk home, Margaret said that there was something she wanted to try and that she would need my help.

"Of course I'll help," I said. Well, we went to her house, and there Margaret said she wanted me to hold her front screen door open while she rode her bicycle down the stairs from the second floor! All the way down the stairs, out onto the porch, down the three porch steps to the front walk and down another three steps to the sidewalk!

I said, "No, I will not!" She would kill herself, I was sure, and I wasn't going to help her. Margaret said no, she wouldn't kill herself. The stairs were lined up with the front door and that would make it easy, she assured me. I started to go home when she said, "If you don't hold it open for me, then I will just have to break it open as I come down the stairs."

I knew Margaret well enough to know she would do just that, so I was in a quandary. She would get hurt worse if the door weren't open. I couldn't talk her out of doing it, and I finally decided she stood a better chance of not getting hurt if I held the door open. She half dragged and half pushed her bicycle to the second floor. When she got it turned around facing the front door, she climbed on and yelled to me, "Open the door, I'm coming down!" I held the door open and began to shake like a leaf— my best friend was about to get killed!

The clattering noise was deafening as she came down the stairs, whizzed past me out the door, off the porch, then off the sidewalk into the street! I realized I had kept my eyes closed during Margaret's wild ride, so I opened them and there she was, sitting on her bike in the middle of the street, perfectly all right. I couldn't believe it!

I heard Mrs. Codding coming up behind me. Of course, Mrs. Codding had heard the awful clatter of the bicycle on the stairs. She saw Margaret in the street and all right and called to her, "Margaret, come in the house—now!" I was frozen to the door, watching Margaret bring her bicycle up on the porch. Then Mrs. Codding looked me straight in the eye and said, "Sydney Burns, I think you'd better go home." I did.

VIII.

A SUMMER EVENING

Sometimes in the evenings after supper we would play croquet. This evening Margaret, Mary Jane and I were playing in my yard. After finishing the game, we sat down a minute on the front porch steps and listened to the crickets and the tree frogs, the sounds of summer, and in a little while the lightning bugs came out, flashing all over the place. Sometimes we caught the little lightning bugs in a jar, after punching holes in the lid so they could breathe.

This night we just walked to the ice cream parlor for ice cream. As usual, we had a hard time deciding what we wanted, I finally decided on a "walking sundae," which was two dips of vanilla ice cream with chocolate sauce, in a cup. Margaret and Mary Jane got chocolate cones.

We walked up the street, eating our ice cream, to see what was playing at the picture show. Mr. and Mrs. Cain, who owned the theater, were good friends of our families and had given us picture show tickets for Christmas. We had already used about half of our tickets on the Westerns that played on Saturdays.

Margaret told us about the Nancy Drew book that she was reading and mentioned that she had heard that a Nancy Drew movie was being made. Mary Jane said we should ask, so we walked over to the ticket window and I said, "Mrs. Cain, we heard they were going to make a Nancy Drew movie, have you heard?"

"No, girls, I haven't, but the next time we go to Cincinnati to see the distributors, I will ask about it."

We walked on up the street and saw a sign on a telephone pole advertising the show boat. It was coming this weekend, and the show was "Uncle Tom's Cabin." We had all read the book so we were excited about seeing the show.

We heard the calliope announcing the boat's arrival as Margaret and I were running errands. We hopped on our bikes and rode to the cobblestone street and then had to stop; our bicycles wouldn't run on the bumpy cobblestones. So we watched the boat dock from afar. We looked on as the deck hands secured the boat and put down the gang plank. We couldn't wait to get home and see when we could go to the show. I rode through my front gate and put up my bicycle. Mother was in the house when I rushed in to tell her about the showboat. She had read *Uncle Tom's Cabin*, too, so she wanted to see the play. She said she would try to get tickets for the opening night and added that she would be happy to take any of my friends, too, if their parents couldn't go.

We walked from home to the cobblestone street, which was only three blocks away. That way we didn't need to worry about parking the car. We walked over the gang plank to the show-boat, and I was so excited! We bought popcorn before we entered the theater and then went inside to find our seats. Mother had gotten good seats—about halfway down and on the aisle. It was thrilling from the time the curtain went up until the play was over and the curtain came down! The applause was really loud. As we walked home, we stopped at the ice cream parlor and got chocolate cones. I ate a lot of ice cream that summer.

IX.

FALLSBURG

In summer one of my favorite things was to go swimming at Fallsburg (if somebody's parents would take us!). Fallsburg was a tiny spot on the road to Ashland, about eight miles north of Louisa. It was named for the falls there, a lovely little waterfall surrounded by a sizable pond with sand all around it. The water was cold and mostly clear to the sandy bottom.

No city pool was ever so enchanting and inviting as this little waterfall. Every weekend all summer we begged our parents to take us swimming. We took towels to sit on the sand and colored inner tubes to float us in the water. We even climbed to the top of the waterfall and sat down, as the water there was shallow and warm. Almost every Sunday after church and lunch we

48

all went to Fallsburg, all except Margaret, who was now spending summers in Cincinnati visiting her aunt.

I missed her a lot, but I didn't miss her correcting my English all the time, just because she was two years older. One day we were walking up the street when I noticed the sign on the train station reading "depot," I turned to her and said, "What is a de-pot?"

She looked at me with her most condescending stare and said, "You will never get into college if you don't learn how to pronounce words! It's not de-pot, that's 'dee-po.' " Well, of course I knew what a "dee-po" was, I just hadn't seen it in writing before.

Then there was the time I was reading aloud to her and came to the word "lingerie," which I pronounced "Ling-er-ree." "That does it," she raved, "when are you going to learn to pronounce words correctly? They'll never let you into college!" Then she said, "It's a French word pronounced 'Lawn-jer-ray' and it means..."

"I know what it means!" I blurted out. "Who wants to go to college anyway!"

When I was just four years old, Aunt Shirley (for a joke) asked me where I was going to college. I told her that I wasn't going to college.

She said, "Why, Sydney Burns, why aren't you going to college?"

I looked at her and said, "You know grandmother wouldn't let me play football!" Ask a foolish question and get a foolish answer!

X.

THE CARNIVAL'S IN TOWN

It was time for the county fair, and the carnival would be coming to town. The fair lasted a week and the carnival would be in town a week. The rides were always set up in the middle of town: the whirl-a-gig was in front of the courthouse, the merry-go-round was in front of the Southern Methodist church, the swings were on a side street beside the court-house, the Ferris wheel was behind the church, and the loop-o-plane and the bingo tent were behind the courthouse.

There were lots of other things, too, like the cotton candy stand and the caramel apple stand and the gypsy fortune teller. It cost 50 cents to get your fortune told, but I preferred to ride the Ferris wheel five times for the same money.

Margaret, Mary Jane, Beth Ann and I met almost every night in front of Rips restaurant, after supper and before dark. We each got 75 cents to spend, which meant we could ride seven times and buy one cotton candy, or we could ride five times and play bingo two times (and maybe win one of those Kewpie dolls covered with rhinestones).

One evening after we had finished supper and I was getting ready to go to the carnival with Mattie, Mabel Loar walked up on our back porch with two pretty little girls about my age. Mabel was a friend of Mattie's and lived in "Need More," which was in the upper end of town, and don't ask where it got its name because I have no idea. A good Christian lady named Pauline, whom everyone called "Aunt Pleen," lived there, too. Mother visited her often and they talked about the Lord. Mother always said that Aunt Pleen had a direct line to heaven.

The two girls with Mabel were from Huntington and had come to spend a week in Louisa. As she introduced us to Becky and Libby Meek, she looked at Mother and said, "They're lawyer Meek's daughters from Huntington." Becky and Libby and I became friends right away and went to the carnival with Mattie and Mabel.

Becky and I loved the rides and rode the Ferris wheel, the merry-go-round and the swings, while Libby spent her money playing bingo. I don't think she moved from the bingo tent from the time we got there to the time we left. Becky and I would come by between rides, but Libby never wanted to go with us to ride anything.

We got some cotton candy and walked around looking at all the people and the sights. We liked watching the Loop-O-Plane the best. All the girls just screamed and screamed as the Loop-O-Plane stood them on their heads and all the loose change in the boys' pockets fell to the ground.

We stopped back again at the bingo tent, and Libby was really excited. She had won a Kewpie doll! The one with the red dress and feather boa around her neck and rhinestone hat and pocket book. Now she was ready to go with us to ride the Ferris wheel.

She clutched that doll like it was worth $100 as she got on the Ferris wheel. The wheel went around once and stopped with us on top. Becky was the more adventurous of the sisters and started to rock the car. That scared Libby so much that she dropped her rhinestone Kewpie doll! Fortunately, it didn't hit anyone, but it did break into a million pieces as it hit the street. As we said goodnight Libby was still crying.

XI.

WINTERTIME

Winter arrived with a quiet that only falling snow can bring. The sun glistened on the new snow, and Louisa, dressed in her white winter gown, became magical. The river was frozen over and people skated across it. The ponds were all frozen. We had to walk everywhere we went. It was almost as if we had been carried back into another century. I was told that once when my grandfather came calling on my grandmother, the river was frozen so he skated from Catlettsburg to Louisa to see her.

It was Saturday, and I was out of school and ready to go sleigh riding. The phone rang and it was Margaret asking when we were going. I said, "You call Beth Ann and I'll call Mary Jane and tell them we'll meet them in half an hour at the hill."

I walked to Margaret's, pulling my sled, and together we walked and pulled our sleds to the town hill beside the grade school. Beth Ann lived almost at the foot of the hill and was already sledding when we got there. Mary Jane arrived soon after. There was a barbed wire fence at the bottom of the hill, but whenever it snowed somebody always cut the barbed wire so we could get to the hill, and if anybody sledded that far down the hill they wouldn't run into the fence. The boys always went to the top of the hill, but we stopped about midway up.

We sledded down the hill until we were tired and frozen and then went into Beth Ann's to get warm. The doorbell rang, and there stood Mother in her snowsuit. She and Beth Ann's mother were going sledding with us.

We all had some hot chocolate and then started up the hill again. Mother rode down the hill on my sled with me in front, and Beth Ann's mother rode down the hill with Beth Ann on her sled. *Whee!* We went farther. We spent the next two hours laughing and sledding and falling off in the snow. Finally, Mother put my and Margaret's sleds in the car trunk and we drove home. Mary Jane lived nearby, so she walked home, and Beth Ann was already home.

Beth Ann's father had a bobsled built that held ten people. On Saturday and Sunday afternoons he would tie the bobsled to his back bumper and take ten of Beth Ann's friends for a sleigh ride. He drove all over town with ten giggling little girls having the time of their lives. He drove slowly so none of us could fall off.

Saturday nights were a different story. He took the adults for a ride on the bobsled. He didn't drive so slowly then. He took the corners pretty fast, but they all had a great time. Afterwards, the group would go to one of their homes and have a late supper. It would be hard to say who had more fun.

A week before Christmas was the time for caroling. The junior choir had been practicing and were ready to go. We always stopped at the shut-ins' first, and then at as many other houses as we could. We sang "Jingle Bells" as we walked through the snow from one house to another; we even had some old sleigh bells that we carried and jingled as we walked along singing. We sang "Silent Night," "It Came Upon a Midnight Clear," "O Come All Ye Faithful," and lots more and enjoyed every minute.

We finally ended at my house, where we took off our heavy clothes and sat down to sandwiches and hot chocolate that Mattie had fixed. After we finished, Mother went to the piano and played "White Christmas" and the "Christmas Song" (chestnuts roasting, etc.) and we all joined in singing. Finally, the evening came to an end and we all hugged each other good night. I wished we could go caroling more than once a year! I would have done it twice a month.

It was the Sunday before Christmas, and Mother's selections for the church choir were beautiful. For one, she asked Ern Compton, who had a lovely bass voice, to sing "O Holy Night." Ern Compton was blind and had only one arm and did not go to church, but always sang when Mother asked him. He had a newspaper stand on the courthouse property, and everyone traded with him. For the anthem the choir sang "The Birthday of the King." During the offertory Mother played Gounod's "Ave Maria" accompanied by the organ and the piano.

The junior choir sang on Sunday night. We had already put our hymnals on our choir chairs so we could come down the aisle carrying lighted candles. The lights in the sanctuary were dimmed so that only the candles on the altar and on the choir railing gave light. There were poinsettias and greenery everywhere; the church looked beautiful. You could have heard a pin drop when we entered singing "It Came Upon a Midnight Clear" in three part harmony. Everyone remarked upon what an impressive service it was.

Christmas day finally came! I was up very early, and both Mother and Mattie were up, too. The presents under the tree looked so colorful, and I couldn't wait to open mine! I got some new clothes, of course, but I also got three new Nancy Drew books, a pretty yellow and gold locket, some new clothes for my doll, and new ice skates! Mattie got a real attractive green wool three-piece suit with two sweaters, and she was more excited than I was. She had brought the large kitchen wastebasket, so we began to fill it with the wrapping paper and the boxes.

Daddy got up then, as he was awakened by all our noise. He opened his gifts while Mattie made breakfast. Mother put on her new red velvet robe that I had given her for Christmas, and we three sat down to breakfast. After breakfast Mattie cleared the table, washed the dishes, and left to spend Christmas with her parents in Fort Gay.

We always had Christmas dinner at Aunt Shirley's—she was the best cook! But then, all my family were good cooks. We three arrived at Aunt Shirley's about two o'clock along with Aunt Lill and Louise Milton. While all the grown-ups were talking, I called Margaret and Mary Jane to see what they had gotten for Christmas. We each had a great Christmas and made plans to go sledding tomorrow.

Aunt Shirley called us to dinner and had darling Christmas place cards for each of us. The dinner was scrumptious—turkey, dressing, gravy, mashed potatoes, candied yams, scalloped oysters, peas, hot rolls (Mattie's), pumpkin pie and walnut cake, and oh, yes, cranberry salad. After dinner we helped carry the dishes to the kitchen, where Sarah would arrive shortly to clean up.

The day was coming to an end as we waddled our way to the car, claiming that we would never eat again! It had been another Christmas to remember. I loved Christmas with my family.

XII.

THE WIFE

While lying on the floor in front of the fire reading *The Big Sandy News*, Margaret and I came across a strange ad in the paper—a man was advertising for a wife! The ad said the woman must be a native-born Kentuckian and like children. Respondents to the ad were directed to a post office box in Portsmouth, Ohio.

We nearly laughed ourselves to death, and then we decided to answer the ad. We couldn't tell our parents, of course; they probably wouldn't think it was so funny, but we did! We had to figure how to do this. We needed a name and address and a description of this "woman." Margaret said, "We should have his answer sent to 'General Delivery' at the post office, and then we could pick it up and he wouldn't have our address." I agreed.

We now had to think of a name and what she looked like. We thought and thought and finally decided she should have strawberry blonde hair and blue eyes and be 25 years old. We figured that was about right. Then we tried lots of names and finally decided to call her Evelyn Keys, General Delivery, Louisa, KY.

Now we were ready. We went to the store and bought some fancy-looking stationery. Margaret had prettier handwriting than I did, so she wrote the letter. We took it to the post office and mailed it, giggling all the way. All we had to do now was wait and see if he answered it.

We waited a couple days and then began to go to the post office to check. It took about a week to get an answer, but then one came. Gosh, that was exciting! We could hardly wait to get home and read it.

The man thought "Evelyn Keys" sounded perfect! He wanted her to come visit him or else he could take a bus and come to see her. We wrote back that we thought he should come and visit her and that he should wear a red flower in his lapel so she would know him.

Now we began to get a little nervous, but calmed ourselves by saying that he wasn't looking for two little girls, but a beautiful young woman with strawberry blonde hair. We didn't hear again for about two weeks. This third letter said he had come to Louisa to find Evelyn Keys, but that nobody he talked to knew her and some people suggested she couldn't be a native-born Kentuckian or they would know. We were so relieved that he had come and gone, and we vowed never to answer such an ad again.

One evening a few nights later my Aunt Shirley invited us over for some cookies. We decided we could tell her about our "letters" and she wouldn't tell on us.

She listened quietly to the whole story, and then she said, "Do you girls know you could have been murdered? That man was probably looking for a pretty young girl to kidnap."

We said, "But he didn't know who we were; he would have looked for a young lady."

My aunt continued, "Did you not think he could have been watching the post office to see who picked up Evelyn Keys' mail?"

"No, ma'am, we never thought of that," I said.

"Well," she said, "if you promise never to do anything like that again, I'll not tell your parents."

"We promise!" we chorused.

I lived only four blocks from Aunt Shirley and Uncle Harry, and Margaret lived only three blocks away, but they had scared us so badly that they had to drive us home. We learned a really good lesson that evening!

XIII.

AUNT SHIRLEY

My Aunt Shirley, my mother's only sister, was an attractive and lovely lady with a marvelous personality and a wonderful talent for painting. She was slender and no taller than 5'1". She had graduated from Mount Saint Joseph Academy, a convent school in Cincinnati, Ohio, where she studied art.

Her china painting was exquisite—so delicate and beautiful. When she was just nineteen years old she painted an entire dinner set of Havilland china—twelve of everything—for my grandmother with my grandmother's initials in gold on each piece.

She was just so talented. She painted baby pillows for her friends who were expecting; she made a pink satin pillow with blue forget-me-nots and a blue satin pillow with pink roses. She also made "combing jackets" for her friends with roses and forget-me-nots. She had her own studio and her own kiln for firing the china. My grandfather liked beer on occasion, so Aunt Shirley painted a large beer stein and eight mugs for him.

But she was interested in more than painting; she founded the Louisa Woman's Club, she organized the Red Cross, and she was also greatly interested in Republican politics. She was a member of the Kentucky Republican Central Committee and served on the State Board of Charities and Corrections. She went on statewide speaking campaigns for the Republican party. The *Lexington Leader* reported, "Mrs. Wellman is one of the most able woman speakers in the state." She was once a delegate to the Republican National Convention, along with my grandfather.

She was also the "Hostess with the Mostest." Her New Year's Day receptions were legendary. She had parties all through the year, and I usually had to assist by meeting her guests at the door (in my black patent leather shoes!). Her house had belonged to the widow of our Revolutionary ancestor. The stairs to the second floor were constructed so that you didn't feel like you were climbing at all. I never minded going upstairs to get something for her like I did going up the stairs at my house.

Aunt Shirley was married but didn't have any children. She was like the rest of the family, though; she had Airedales, two of them—a boy named Pat and girl named Patsy. She had hoped to raise Airedales, but that didn't happen. They wouldn't mate.

When she bought the dogs she had a cyclone fence put around her property. Her house was only a block from the river, and Pat and Patsy sneaked off all the time to swim in the river. Nobody could figure how they got out of the fence until Aunt Shirley was looking out the window one day and saw how they did it. Pat would stand up at the gate and take his paw and punch down the catch that opened the gate, and Patsy would push the gate open. Then off they would go for a swim!

They were like a couple of clowns and always kept us amused with their antics. They were sweet and friendly too; the whole family loved them.

Tragedy struck poor Pat, though. It was time for his annual rabies shot. There was a veterinarian in Louisa, so Aunt Shirley took her dogs there for their shots. (We took Sandy to Ashland for his shots.)

Patsy got along just fine, but the day after Pat had his shot, he became paralyzed from the neck down! If you have never seen a paralyzed animal, you cannot imagine the horror and devastation you can see in its eyes as it tries to move. Pat couldn't understand why he couldn't move anything but his head, and he kept moving his poor head constantly for the first day.

My grandfather advised and almost insisted that Aunt Shirley have Pat "put down," but she wouldn't hear of it. She had a cot put into her guest bedroom for him to lie on. She would lift his head and shoulders and hold him up so he could eat a little or get a drink of water.

The strangest thing, almost eerie, happened every morning. Patsy would come to the door of the guest room and stand there, and then she and Pat would talk to each other with low, gutteral sounds for about five minutes. Patsy would leave after their morning ritual and not come back to see Pat again until the next day.

Finally, though, Pat died. No animal ever had better care, but all the family thought that Aunt Shirley should have had Pat "put down." If that had happened to Sandy, I don't know what I would have done! Patsy missed him so much, you could tell, but she lived a normal lifespan for an Airedale.

Daddy taught me that if you loved your animals, you looked after them, and that included not letting them suffer when they couldn't get well. But I knew, too, that Aunt Shirley really loved Pat.

XIV.

A VERY GREAT LOSS

Mother woke me in the middle of the night with terrible news. She shook me gently and said, "Honey, wake up, Daddy's gone."

I didn't understand, I jumped out of bed and answered, "We have to go find him!"

Then she softly said, "No, honey, he's gone to heaven." I began to sob. My beloved grandfather was gone! Then I heard our dog Sandy on our back porch, howling and howling; he knew "Daddy" was gone, and he was crying too.

It was too much; no more walks uptown for ice cream, no more stories of Ring and Willie, and no more holding his hand as we walked to church. I had met him in the upstairs hall just the night before, as I was on my way to the bathroom to undress. I reached up my arms and

68

he leaned down so I could kiss him good-night and he said, "Ahh, boy! That's the best kiss I've had all day."

There was a lot of love between the two of us. I was heartbroken. I thought people had to be sick to die. I didn't know you could have a heart attack and die quickly. It was hard for a ten-year-old to understand. Mother told me that he had called her and she went running in and he told her he had bad chest pains. She had run to call the doctor, and when she got back he was gone.

The next few days were so busy, people coming and going all day and night, and mountains of food arriving. We kept my grandfather at home, in our music room, and I spent most of the next three days in there with him. I wasn't hungry, and I didn't sleep very well. I came upon Mother leaning over on the mantel in the living room, head on her arms, crying, and I didn't know what to do so I left her alone.

My Aunt Shirley and my Great-Aunt Lillian were there all day every day. All the townspeople came to pay their respects, and a group of the men from our church came to see Mother and Aunt Shirley to talk them out of having the funeral at home (my grandmother's had been at home). These men told Mother and Aunt Shirley that our house wouldn't hold the people who would come.

Mother and Aunt Shirley then decided to have his funeral at the Southern Methodist church. Dr. Frederick Shannon, who had been born and reared in Louisa and was an old friend of my grandfather, would conduct the funeral. Dr. Shannon lived in Chicago and was the pastor of one of the largest churches in Chicago and filled a pulpit in London for a month during the summer. He was greatly saddened by my grandfather's death and would be a great comfort to Mother.

The day of the funeral dawned bright with sunshine. The funeral home car arrived to take us to the church. All the businesses in town, as well as the courthouse and the post office, were closed during the funeral because my grandfather was a much-beloved and respected man.

Right before the funeral began, one of the pallbearers lifted me up to the casket, and I took one red rose out of Daddy's lapel and put in a fresh one. Daddy always wore a fresh rose, every day. The choir sang and Daddy's favorite soprano, Emily Young, sang his favorite hymn, "His Eye is on the Sparrow." Its next line is, "so I know he watches me." How often had Daddy told me that!

The men from the church were right about the funeral being in the church. There were so many people at the funeral they couldn't all get in the church. People lined up on the church steps and the sidewalk outside. The great number of people was a fine tribute to my grandfather.

After the funeral the cortege went through town and up the hill to the cemetery. My grandfather had selected a beautiful spot where the whole town could be seen, and had had a mausoleum built there. My grandmother was buried there, and my grandfather was to be put beside her. The other places were for Aunt Shirley and her husband and mother and me. My grandfather always said that the first person he wanted to see on Resurrection Day was me.

After we left the cemetery we went home, where lots of friends and family joined us. Our housekeeper, Mattie, with help from the other cooks in town, was busy fixing dinner for all the out-of-town friends and family. After dinner Mother and I told everyone goodbye and prepared to begin life without my grandfather.

Our wonderful housekeeper, Mattie, came into the living room with a suitcase and said, "I know you girls don't want to be alone, so I'm moving in to live with you." We were so pleased and surprised at her thoughtfulness. We cried, "Yes! Yes! Yes!" We had plenty of room, so she could have her own room and bath—we had six bedrooms, and Mother and I only used two of them.

Our lives would never be the same. We would always miss my beloved grandfather.

XV.

THE RIVER

School was out, and I was looking forward to playing outside again. Sandy and I were sitting on the front porch steps together; he was panting and I was eating a popsicle. In other words, summer was back. Sandy seemed so hot that I decided he needed to cool off with a swim in the river—never mind that I wasn't allowed near the river.

Sandy and I walked to Margaret's to see if she wanted to go, and of course she did. We couldn't go down the cobblestone street to the river because too many people would see us and call our parents. We decided to go between houses and sneak down to the riverbank and hope no one would spot us.

When we got to the river, we saw a rowboat

72

on the bank with a rope stretched around a big tree. Margaret climbed in the back and I climbed in the front, and Sandy jumped in the river with gusto. At last he was cool and was swimming around close to us.

All of a sudden I felt the boat move. I looked up at the tree and saw the rope sliding down the bank. It hadn't been tied up at all! I screamed, "Jump, Margaret!" as I leaped out onto the muddy bank. We both got out, and we were both muddy. Sandy climbed out when we did. We turned around just in time to see the boat disappear behind some overhanging bushes! The current was pulling it toward the dam.

What could we do? If it went over the dam, the boat would break into a million pieces, and we didn't even know who owned it. We had to get to a phone quickly and call the lockmaster (although what he could do, we didn't know).

We washed off the mud as best we could and ran to find a phone. We stopped at a grocery store and borrowed theirs. We got the lockmaster and told him about the boat. That is when we learned that the boat had never made it to the dam; it had gotten hung up on some more overhanging bushes. We never told our parents about our escapade, and we never went near the river again.

XVI.

THE GIFT

After my grandfather died, Mother and Aunt Shirley wanted to do something to honor my grandparents. My great-grandfather, Judge John M. Burns, who had lived in Ashland, Kentucky, had given land, located in the middle of downtown Ashland, to build a Baptist church. My family had always been proud of him for doing that. Now Mother and Aunt Shirley had a chance to do something for God and honor my grandparents. Our church had a concert grand piano but no organ, so Mother thought they could give an organ to the church in memory of my grandparents.

She looked and listened for weeks at different organs and then decided on a Hammond. She thought it had the best sound, and its keyboard allowed for all sorts of variations in sound. There were other organs that were similar, but the Hammond was the top of the line.

Mother and Aunt Shirley sent invitations to friends and relatives both in town and out of town. The congregation of the Southern Methodist church was invited from the pulpit the Sunday before the dedication.

The organ was dedicated on Sunday, July 10, at 3 p.m. That date was the 50th wedding anniversary of my grandparents. The organ prelude was played by Mr. Val Heisel of Portsmouth, Ohio. The invocation was given by Rev. Sherwood W. Funk, pastor of the Southern Methodist church. The organ recital was played by Mr. Charles E. Sherman, organist of the Second Presbyterian church in Portsmouth, Ohio. The program included these pieces:

Choral No.3 in A minor, by Caesar Franch
Prelude : Lohengrim, by Wagner
Toccato and Fugue in D minor, by Bach
Prelude and Fugue on the name B-A-C-H,
    by Liszt
Toccata Fifth Symphony, by Charles M.
    Widor

About 250 people attended the dedication and the reception afterwards at Aunt Shirley's house. Mother and Aunt Shirley had close friends assist in the dining room, where punch, tea sandwiches, and tea cakes were served. I helped welcome the guests (wearing my black patent leather shoes, of course!) There were small tables scattered around the lawn surrounding Aunt Shirley's house where the guests could sit down and enjoy the refreshments.

It was a wonderful day that I'll always remember.

Southern Methodist Church, Louisa, Kentucky

XVII.

THE HOUSE PARTY

On a beautiful summer day Mother came and told me that I could have a house party and invite my Virginia cousins for a week! That would be more fun than a barrel of monkeys! Now I had to write and see if they could come.

My Virginia cousins were the great-great-grandchildren of my great-great-uncle, William Harvey Burns, who was the brother and law partner of my great-grandfather, John M. Burns. They had an office together in West Liberty, Kentucky, but at the beginning of the Civil War, great-great- Uncle William moved to Lebanon, Virginia. Southern cousins, as you can see, "claim kin" for generations. We call them "kissin' cousins."

My cousins, Elkanah (named for his grandfather), Eula Carroll, his sister, and our mutual cousin, Bobby Burns, could all come for the week. They would be coming on Saturday on the N & W train, which stopped across the river in Fort Gay, West Virginia. For an only child, this was like having transparent pie and a hot fudge sundae all rolled into one.

Mother and I met the train on Saturday in Fort Gay. Bobby, Eula Carroll, and Caney got off, and the boys carried their luggage to our car.

By the time they got settled in their rooms and bathed, supper was ready. Mattie had fixed my favorite supper—fried chicken, mashed potatoes and gravy, creamed peas, corn pudding, hot rolls and transparent pie.

After we ate we went out in the yard and played a few games of croquet. The boys against the girls, of course! We talked a blue streak and then went to bed.

The next day was Sunday, so we went to Sunday school and church with Mother. After lunch she drove us to Fallsburg to go swimming; the boys hadn't seen a waterfall like that before and couldn't wait to climb to the top and look down (you know boys!). Eula Carroll and I played in the pond and sat on our towels on the sand, while the boys spent their time crawling all over the rocks atop the waterfall. We had a great time and hated to leave, but it was almost supper time.

We rode home, took our baths and got ready for supper. Mattie fixed another wonderful meal, plus some more transparent pie. Again we went out into the yard to play croquet and played until dark. Since it was too early to go to bed, we went in the house and played Monopoly until bedtime.

Louisa now had two drugstores but only one druggist. The newer one had a soda fountain, some gift stuff and a juke box! There was a large floor where we could dance and tables around the floor where we could sit and have ice cream or Cokes. The young people danced, and the older people sat around and visited with one another.

My Virginia cousins loved to dance, and so did I! So every night after supper we headed for Atkins and Vaughn's Drugstore to dance. It was only two blocks from my house, so we walked. Bobby was the best dancer and I loved to dance with him, but Eula Carroll didn't want to dance with her brother all the time, so I had to share him. Bobby was older than we were, so we all looked up to him.

Mother took us to swim at Dreamland Pool in Huntington, West Virginia. It had two slides, three diving boards, and two floats in the middle. Tables with colored umbrellas surrounded one side, and everything was in pastel colors. It was a beautiful pool that looked like something out of a Technicolor movie.

That week went by so fast; we had played croquet, swum, and danced every night and had had the best fun ever, but the time had come for them to go home. But before they were to leave, Eula Carroll's mother called and invited me to come home with them for a week! I was really excited!

I got on the train with them in Fort Gay, and Mattie had packed a lunch for us to eat on the way—ham biscuits, fried chicken, deviled eggs and fudge. We let the train pull out of the station before we opened the box!

We got off in Bluefield, Virginia, and Bobby's oldest brother, Budley, met us at the train. Lebanon had no train, so Bluefield was the closest station. It took us about an hour to drive to Lebanon.

Eula Carroll's mother had planned a party in my honor, so I had brought my prettiest summer dress to wear. I think everybody in Lebanon was invited, and it was a beautiful evening. Lebanon was in the mountains and the evenings were cooler than at home.

I got dressed and Eula Carroll and I went downstairs together to meet the guests. Eula Carroll was introducing me to her friends when one of the girls called me aside and told me that my hair looked so pretty and wondered if I had had it done at the beauty shop. I said, "No, I did it myself." She looked sweetly at me and replied, "I didn't know you were old enough to comb your own hair."

After my first experience with catty girls, I decided I liked boys better. That girl thought Bobby was her sweetheart and I was somehow in the way. I didn't know how to answer her; I was mad and embarrassed, so I just walked away. Bobby danced a lot more with me than he did with her, but I never told him what she had said.

We spent a day at Hungry Mother State Park, another day shopping in Bristol, and lots of evenings at Bobby's house, "Breezy Hill." His father, Cousin Clarence, was a lawyer and told wonderful stories like Daddy used to. They were first cousins, so I guess it ran in the family.

XVIII.

SANDY

I was awake but not out of bed when Mother came rushing up the stairs calling my name. I jumped out of bed and met her in the hall. She was crying as she told me that Sandy had been poisoned! My best friend and constant companion was gone! Who would be so mean? None of my friends were afraid of him. I was heartbroken.

I remembered when Daddy had taken me to help pick out a puppy. I was just a little girl and so excited to get a puppy. We went to an Airedale kennel in Ashland, Kentucky, where we saw a mother and six little puppies. My grandfather told me to watch the puppies play and see which one was the most active and which one the mother seemed to like the best, and that would be the pick of the litter and the one we wanted.

We watched for about twenty minutes, and then we both picked "Sandy." He was only six weeks old and cute as could be. It took about an hour to drive home, and Sandy snuggled in my lap all the way. We grew up together and were never far apart.

All these memories came rushing back and made me heartsick. After Daddy had died, Sandy had slept upstairs with us at night. Whenever we awakened we could hear his toenails clicking on the hardwood floors as he walked all over the upstairs, trying to be on guard for us. It made us feel safe and comforted.

I asked Mother if we could get a casket for him, and she told me that they didn't make dog caskets but that she would call the lumber company and have them make one. The "casket" came at noon, and I covered the inside with pink material—my favorite color. Then I got my favorite blue hair ribbon and put it around Sandy's neck.

My Aunt Shirley came to conduct the funeral, and when all my friends arrived, parking their bicycles on the patio, she began. She stood beside the casket and prayed, "Dear Lord, today we are sending you our beloved dog, Sandy. He was as faithful and loyal as any dog could be. We know you love animals, for you made them, and we know that heaven would not be heaven without the birds singing and the animals playing around your feet. We know that Sandy will be happy there and ask that you look after him for us. Amen."

Our yard man had dug a grave under the cherry tree, where Sandy used to lie in the summertime. It was out of the way of the croquet court, but where I could see it every day. The sky was blue, the day was bright, and the sun was warm. No different from yesterday, when Sandy was still here and sitting on the porch beside me. I would miss him terribly, but I knew that he and Daddy would be happy together.

School had started again, but I still missed Sandy; even starting junior high school didn't help my sadness to go away. One day in October while I was reading the paper, *The Herald-Dispatch* from Huntington, West Virginia (we took the Ashland, Kentucky paper, too, but in the evening), I saw an article that said you could win a dog if you won this essay contest.

I planned right then to enter the contest. My only problem was that I didn't know what an essay was. I would ask Mother, but I wouldn't tell her about the contest. She told me that an essay was several paragraphs or several pages, depending on the length of the essay, about a single subject.

I thought about all the reasons why I wanted a dog, particularly an Airedale, and began to write them down. I worked on it after school for several days. Finally, I put it together and wrote as neatly as I could and mailed it.

What would happen, I wondered? I just had to win, but there would be so many girls and boys entering the contest that I probably didn't stand a chance.

One day about a month later while I was home for lunch, the phone rang. Mattie answered it and the person asked for Mother, but she was out. Mattie asked if she could take a message. The man on the phone asked if there were a "Master Sydney Burns Lindsey" living there. Mattie said, "No 'Master,' but a Miss Sydney Burns Lindsey." He said I had won first prize in *The Herald-Dispatch* essay contest and he would call back later and talk to Mother. Mattie put down the phone and turned to me and said, "Did you enter an essay contest in the paper?"

I screamed, "Yes! Yes! What did they say?"

She looked at me and answered, "You won the contest!"

I couldn't believe it, I said, "Are you sure?"

"That's what the gentleman said, and also

that he would call back and talk to your mother. And oh, yes." She started laughing. "He thought you were a boy!"

I could hardly contain my excitement. I went hopping all over the house singing, "I won! I won! I won!" I had a hard time waiting for Mother to get home. She came home right before I started back to school.

"Mother," I cried, "remember when I asked you what an essay was?"

She said, "Yes, I remember."

"Well, I entered an essay contest in *The Herald-Dispatch* and won first prize."

"You did what?"

"I entered an essay contest and won first prize and won a dog!"

She was flabbergasted. She said, "You have won a dog? Come here and let me hug you!"

We hugged and danced all over the room. The gentleman from the newspaper called back in the afternoon and talked with Mother. We were to be in Huntington at Vanity Fair on Saturday night, where my essay would be read over the radio and I would have my picture taken for *The Herald-Dispatch* and be pre-sented with my dog.

How exciting! But all I really wanted was my dog. Saturday was the opening day of the Kennel Club's all-breed dog show at Vanity Fair. The Huntington Kennel Club had co-sponsored the contest with the Herald-Dispatch.

Mother and I left early Saturday evening so we would have plenty of time to get to Huntington and have spaghetti for dinner at Jim's Spaghetti House before going to Vanity Fair. Jim's spaghetti was my favorite, and Mother and I always ate there on the nights we drove to Huntington for the Marshall Artist series. I wore my favorite party dress, which was light blue, and my black patent leather shoes (even though I still didn't like them).

Mother sat in the audience while I sat on the front row with the other winners. Since I had won first prize, my essay was read first. I had to stand on the stage while my essay was read by Wyatt Smith, managing editor of *The Herald-Dispatch*. Fortunately it wasn't too long, as Mother had told me to stand still and not fidget.

After my essay reading, I was presented with my dog by Harvey Taylor Jr., who represented the Kennel Club. She was a rust-and-black-colored Airedale. I named her "Rusty" at first sight. She was a very friendly dog, and I knew we would get along just fine. In my heart, though, she wasn't Sandy and never would be.

XIX.

CAN I STAY HOME?

When I came home from school, I saw Aunt Shirley's car parked out front. I hurried in because I always loved to see her. She and Mother were talking when I walked in and threw my books on the hall table as I said, "Hey, I'm home!"

They both laughed and said, "We heard you." Mother continued, "Come and sit down; we want to talk to you." I hugged them both and then sat down beside Mother on the sofa.

Mother started, "You know that Aunt Shirley and I went away to boarding school when we were your age." I was so unprepared for this that I was speechless! Aunt Shirley continued, "We think it's time for you to go away to school, too."

Tears stung my eyes as I blinked and cried, "Please, I don't want to go away to school, I want to stay here!" I looked at Mother. "You'd be all alone, except for Mattie, if I left."

Aunt Shirley spoke up. "It's for your good, you'll get a better education this way."

"I don't care, I want to stay home. College will be soon enough to leave." By this time I was really crying. They both said that we could discuss it at another time.

As Aunt Shirley left she put her arm around me and said, "You know it would be as hard for us to let you go as it would be for you to leave. We are only thinking of what's best for you." I nodded and went upstairs.

How could I have NOT known? I was the age to go away, but I didn't want to! I'd only been a majorette for a year, and I loved being in the band; I made the honor roll every month; I was the president of the Youth Fellowship at church, and I sang in the choir, too. My life was here in Louisa—at least until I graduated.

Mother and I sat down to supper and didn't talk very much, and I didn't eat very much. After supper I got my lessons for the next day while Mother read. When we both finished we went upstairs to get ready for bed. I got my night clothes on, brushed my teeth, washed my face and went to Mother's room to say good-night.

I couldn't stand it one minute longer, I began to cry again and begged Mother not to send me away to school. She had tears in her eyes as she said, "I don't want you to be unhappy, and I would miss you so! Just because we went away to boarding school doesn't mean that you have to."

"Then I can stay home?" I ventured.

"Of course you can. I'll tell Aunt Shirley our decision tomorrow."

I went to bed happy. "Home" had never seemed dearer.

XX.

A MOMENTUS OCCASION

Mother had been getting lots of attention since my grandfather had died. She was very popular and had lots of dates. There was a surgeon from Washington, D. C., who came quite often to call on her. She had known him when she was younger. He met Mother and Aunt Shirley and Uncle Harry in New York to see the new Broadway plays. I wished I were older so I could go! I loved plays.

The one I liked the best was Mr. Vinson (a first cousin of Chief Justice Fred Vinson). He sometimes helped me with my lessons (when Mother was late!) and played Chinese checkers with me and took me out to dinner with them. It was Mr. Vinson that she decided to marry after seeing several nice men for a couple of years.

Louise Milton and her husband, Wes Ballard, were their attendants. They were married in the Southern Methodist church with all their friends and relatives in attendance. I lit the candles in the large candelabras that stood in front of the altar. I got a new white dress to wear and NO BLACK PATENT LEATHER SHOES. I got to wear new white ones!

After the ceremony, as they were leaving the church, we got separated. I could see them getting to the car with everyone throwing rice. I was on the top step of the church steps and I called to Mother, "Wait for me, Mother!"

Everyone turned around and burst out laughing. They didn't know that I was driving part way with them on their honeymoon. They were taking me to Vanceburg, Kentucky, to stay with my cousin, Rachael Johnson, while they were away. I could have stayed at home, of course, with Mattie and all my relatives in town, but I wanted to visit Rachael; we always had so much fun together. We visited each other every summer. Her grandmother lived in Louisa, so we saw each other often in Louisa. My grandfather and her grandmother were first cousins; when my grandfather began to practice law he practiced with Rachael's great-grandfather in Louisa.

We should have arrived in Vanceburg in about two hours, but we had a flat tire on the road, in the middle of nowhere, and Mr. Vinson had to change the tire (in his good clothes!). It took about an hour longer to get to Vanceburg. Mother and Mr. Vinson didn't stay long at Rachael's, after a short visit with Cousin Doris and Cousin Sam (Rachael's parents), they were off to Columbus, Ohio, for the night and then Canada.

I was so exited to be at Rachael's. I just loved Cousin Doris and Cousin Sam. He was such fun and did such funny things to make us laugh. Cousin Doris played the organ for church and was so pretty and sweet.

Rachael had an older brother named Camp who was good-looking but never paid any attention to us. He didn't bother to speak to us most of the time. Boys! They sure could be a trial sometimes.

The most fun we had was having a picnic and swimming in Kinniconnich creek. "Kinnie" was a large creek that flowed directly into the Ohio River. It had an Indian name from a long-ago tribe. Cousin Doris had fixed sandwiches and potato salad, deviled eggs and lemonade, and some cookies for dessert. We swam for a long time in the creek. It had shallow water and very deep water and was fun to play in. Cousin Sam and Cousin Doris swam with us, and since we could all swim, too, we were always safe.

Ginger, their blonde cocker spaniel, had pups while I was there, five darling little blonde babies. But like my kittens, we couldn't touch them, just look at them. Ginger seemed so proud of them, and I wanted one, but when I asked Mother (she called from Canada), she said that we had enough pets.

It was time for Mother's honeymoon to be over, and they were due to pick me up tomorrow. I was anxious to see Mother, but I hated to leave my cousins. I had had a wonderful time.

Mother and Mr. Vinson arrived at Rachael's about two o'clock in the afternoon. After another brief visit with Rachael and her folks, we started home. Mother and Mr. Vinson had a wonderful time in Canada and had lots of pictures to show me. I didn't have any pictures (I had forgotten my camera!), but I had sure had a good time with my cousins.

XXI.

HOW ABOUT A WEENIE ROAST?

At least once a summer Mattie took all my friends and me on a weenie roast. There were about an even number of girls and boys; we were now teenagers, and we enjoyed doing things in a mixed group. The two boys who lived across the street from me, Bobby and David, were my good friends and always went. We walked to school together, too.

We each took what we wanted to eat—hot dogs, potato chips, pickles, mustard, and for dessert, marshmallows. Mattie fixed a large Thermos jug of lemonade, and one of the boys carried it.

We walked up the town hill, and at the top the trail divided. To the right was the old reservoir, which was nothing but a huge rectangular hole in the ground lined with cement; and to the left was the new reservoir, which was the real reservoir that held the water for Louisa. It was really tall and had a ladder on the side that went to the top. Mattie had a time keeping the boys from climbing atop the reservoir—even telling them they couldn't come with us next time if they disobeyed her.

The first thing we did was to find a large level spot where we could build a fire and sit around it. Next, we looked for enough wood to make a fire, and finally we looked for long, sturdy sticks to poke through our hot dogs and marshmallows so they could cook over the open fire. As we all started out to search for these things, Mattie always said the same thing: "Everybody stay in plain sight where I can see you. Nobody goes over the hill to look for anything!" We all had great respect for Mattie and did as we were told. She was a lot of fun and laughed at all our jokes, but when she spoke she meant business.

The boys built the fire, a big one, and we started putting our hot dogs on the sticks. We held our sticks over the fire until the hot dogs were done or burnt, whichever came first. The boys' dogs usually ended up burnt and the girls' just done. We pulled the hot dogs off the sticks with the hot dog buns. Then we smeared mustard all over them. Nothing ever tasted quite as

good as a burned hot dog smothered in mustard!
I usually ate two and the boys ate three.

By this time it was beginning to get dark,
and we started to toast our marshmallows over
the fire. Talk about burnt—the marshmallows
really got burnt! In fact, some of us would catch
our marshmallows on fire on purpose and then
blow out the fire, and the marshmallows would
be perfect on the inside, if a little black on the
outside.

When we were all full and out of jokes we
would sing awhile. We loved to sing "Row, Row,
Row Your Boat." The first five would start
singing, and when they reached the word "boat"
the second five would start at the beginning,
then the third five and finally the last five.
That was such a fun song to do in a round, and
we always enjoyed it.

By this time it was dark, so we put out the
fire with dirt and the boys stomped on it so we
were sure it was out before we left. We made
our way down the hill by moonlight, talking and
laughing all the way. As we walked home, friends
kept dropping out to go to their homes. By the
time we got to my street there were only four
of us left: Bobby, David, Mattie and me. The
boys thanked Mattie for taking us, and we
parted in front of my house. Mattie was such a
good sport and always happy to take us on
weenie roasts.

XXII.

MARGARET GRADUATES

I couldn't believe the time had come for Margaret and me to separate. I would miss my friend so much! She had been away for the summers for several years now, but always came home in time for school. Now she would be gone all winter and all summer too, since she wanted to finish college in three years.

Mary Jane had moved away three years ago, so I seemed to be losing my friends one at a time. But M. J. moved only to Catlettsburg. We still saw each other when she came to visit her grandparents, who still lived in Louisa.

As you can guess, my friend Margaret was her class valedictorian. I guess all those plays we wrote and all the perfume and soap we sold finally paid off. Oh, and yes, she pronounced all her words correctly, so she was indeed going to college!

Margaret got all the other honors that the valedictorian receives and accepted everything gracefully. No one would ever guess now that she was my co-conspirator who answered letters from a man seeking a wife in the classifieds and hurtled her bicycle down her front stairs. From now on, though, we had to be "grown-ups." What a drag!

Margaret gave a wonderful address, and her family was justly proud of her, as were my family and I. In a few weeks we would be saying goodbye again, but as long as her family stayed in Louisa we would still see each other.

The summer was hot, and I was glad I wasn't going away to school like Margaret. I had a badminton court in my yard now, but it was too hot to play in the daytime so we played in the early evening. Then my step-father had the court lighted so we could play after dark when it was cooler. We played every night, and Mother kept Cokes in the refrigerator for us. It was a lovely, lovely summer.

XXIII.

WE DID ALL OF THIS IN A DAY—
BUT THEN, WE WERE TEENAGERS

I had now moved from the junior choir to the senior choir. They practiced every Thursday night at the church. It was fun, and I had always loved singing. My friends Jimmy and Mark Lackey, Bill McNabb, Joe Carter and Bob Stewart all sang in the choir and sat in the row directly behind me.

One Sunday morning during the summer, I took off my shoes while the minister was preaching. The shoes didn't hurt, but it was hot and it just felt good to be barefooted. When the sermon was over and the choir stood to sing the last hymn, I couldn't find my shoes! I felt around but still couldn't find them; then I turned around to look at the boys behind me.

They all looked like little angels holding their hymnals and singing and not looking at me. Then I knew: they had taken my shoes. I whispered to them to give them back, but they just kept singing. When the service was over I had to march out with the choir in my bare feet!

We walked to the choir room in the basement to take off our robes, and I found Jimmy had my shoes stuffed in his pants pockets under his robe. He ran out of the basement and upstairs carrying my shoes, with me close behind. We were outside the church on the sidewalk before I realized it. All the people were visiting as usual, and there I was barefooted in my Sunday dress. Then the boys were throwing my shoes back and forth over my head so I couldn't reach them.

All the people standing around began laughing (I guess they thought "you can put teenagers in solemn services but you can't put the solemn services in the teenagers!"). I started to laugh, and the boys were already laughing. They finally gave my shoes back (but were my feet ever dirty by then!) and we made plans to go swimming at Fallsburg after lunch.

The boys came by around one-thirty and picked me up and then picked up the other girls. The car was jammed full with all of us. Fallsburg was only eight miles away, so it didn't take long to get there. We jumped out of the car and rushed to the sand beach, put down our towels and other junk, and then ran to the pond and dived in.

The cold water felt so good. We swam around, splashed a lot and climbed to the top of the "falls." We stood there and looked down at the pond and felt the warm, shallow water running over our feet. What a perfect day it was!

We finally climbed down and swam back to the sandy beach. We sat down on our towels and talked about going to the MYF meeting at seven o'clock. I had to play the pump organ while Jimmy pumped. Our hymn singing was limited to certain hymns, since I could only play the ones in the key of B flat or the key of C.

I decided that it was a perfect time to ask the boys about dancing. I cleared my throat and said, "How about everybody coming to my house after the MYF meeting and we'll roll up the rugs and practice dancing?" They all said yes, they'd like that. I had gotten a record player for my birthday and had lots of "danceable" records.

Tired from swimming, we made our way back to town singing lustily. We pulled up in front of "Rips," and our group of sunburned faces climbed out for a Coke. The boys dropped us at home and we all got ready for supper.

We met again at seven for the MYF meeting. After the meeting was over we all walked to my house. Jimmy and Mark rolled up the rugs in the living room, while the other boys moved the furniture back so we could dance. I had my record player on a table with all my records.

The time had come! We put on a slow number and each of us girls picked out a boy to teach to dance. We started them with the "two step," two steps to the right and then two steps to the left, in time to the tempo of the music. The boys got the hang of it in a little while and enjoyed learning to dance.

They enjoyed it so much, in fact, that Mother had to come in and laughingly tell us that the dance floor was closed for the evening. We had been dancing for over two hours! She also told us that if the boys all learned to dance she would let me have a dance on my birthday. Were we ever excited! As far as we were concerned it was a "done deal!"

We decided we would teach the boys the box step next Sunday night. By the time summer was over the boys could all dance like a wonder.

XXIV.

EVER PAINTED A CAR?

In between swimming and learning to dance, Bob Stewart had talked his parents into buying a car for him—not just any car, and certainly not this year's model, but a Model A Ford convertible! I guess you'd call it a convertible; it didn't have a top.

Bob was so excited, and he and his friend James Hager (the son of the Baptist minister) started to work on the car right away. The motor needed lots of work to get it going, and it was badly in need of a paint job.

I stopped to see how things were going and saw that Bob and James were painting the car yellow. It looked really sharp; the yellow was nice and bright. I suggested they paint red circles all over it so that it looked polka-dotted.

They looked at me to see if I were joking, and when they saw that I wasn't, they said very condescendingly, "And just how would we do that, if we wanted to?"

So I told them. "You get your compass and draw perfect circles all over the car. When you get them all drawn, then you paint the circles red and you have a polka-dotted car, and nobody else would have one like it."

Bob looked at James and said, "I think I like it, let's do it."

James replied, "Okay, but let her draw the circles." That's how I got to help paint the car.

We had to let the yellow paint dry before I could draw the circles. It dried overnight, so the next day I began drawing the circles. When I finished we all three started painting them red. Somewhere during the process Bob decided to name the car "Umbriago." Where he got the name I'll never know, but it was his car, after all.

We had lots of fun all summer riding all over town with our friends jammed in the seats. Bob picked us up in the evenings and then we would go and park in front of "Rips." We'd sit there and enjoy Coke floats. We just couldn't go out of town in it, in case it rained.

XXV.

MY TEA DANCE

It was November, and true to her word, Mother was giving me a tea dance for my sixteenth birthday. The boys could all dance now. We planned on having a grand time.

Mother wrote the invitations on her "calling cards" and sent them to all my friends and some of her older friends (friends of my grandparents, really). The older ladies were invited to come later than my friends and included my Cousin Elizabeth, Cousin Thursa (first cousins of my grandfather), Aunt Lill, Mrs. Jennie Hughes (Jim's and Mark's grandmother), Mrs. Emma Turner, and Mrs. Hermia Northrup.

We had floor-to-ceiling sliding doors between the living room and the music room. The rugs were taken up in the living room and the furniture moved back against the walls, which left a large area in the middle for dancing. My record player would be on a table in the corner along with all my records. The older ladies would sit in the music room, where they could visit and watch the dancing. French doors from the living room opened into the dining room, where the table would be set with my grandmother's tea service, tea sandwiches and my birthday cake.

The day finally arrived, and I was surely excited! I had a new black velvet dress to wear and new black shoes—but not patent leather. Those were finally gone forever!

My guests all arrived (the party was from three o'clock to six o'clock), and it was time to start the music. I put on the first record and turned around to see who would be the first on the floor. Was I ever surprised! The boys wouldn't dance! All these boys who had danced with us every week after MYF meeting were now too self-conscious to get out on the floor. The record ended and nobody had danced! My party was a big flop!

I put on another record and walked up to my friend Bobby, who lived across the street, and asked him to dance. He refused. As I walked back to the record player I felt someone tap me on the shoulder. I turned around and there stood Harold, Bobby's cousin. "May I have this dance?" he said.

At last! I gave him my biggest smile and answered "Yes, and thank you."

We were only alone on the dance floor about a minute when everyone got up and danced. The boys had just been waiting for someone else to do it first! Nobody sat down for two hours; once they got started they wouldn't stop.

Mother finally invited us into the dining room for tea or punch, sandwiches and a very large cake with "Sweet Sixteen" written on it. She thought my friends would enjoy punch more than tea, but she was mistaken—all my friends took tea. They were invited to a tea dance, so they were going to drink tea! Aunt Shirley served the tea and was delighted that the young people drank tea. Mother served the punch and got no business at all except from me; I hated tea!

Mattie kept the table filled and enjoyed seeing all the young people she had taken on wiener roasts now dressed up in their Sunday best. My guests danced way past six o'clock, and I had a wonderful happy birthday.

XXVI.

FOOTBALL AND BASKETBALL

We had one football game left before Thanksgiving. My friend Bobby was captain of the football team, and my cute friend Betty Lou was a cheerleader. We had all been in the same room since the first grade and were all good friends and often walked to school together.

Our last football game was with Paintsville, our biggest rival. It was a sunny fall day and the bleachers were full. Betty Lou led the cheers and the band played and marched at halftime. I was no longer in the band; as Mother had said, "You're too old to wear a dress that short!"

We lost the game and we were all crushed. The team had played so hard. We girls went to "Rips" to wait for the football players to shower, change and meet us there. They were a sad bunch when they finally arrived, and they didn't feel like dancing. Bobby bought two chocolate sodas for us and then walked me home. Maybe next year.

Basketball season began not too long after football season ended. A few games were before Christmas, but most were after. Almost the same boys played basketball that played football (small school). We had three high schools in the county, so no school was very large, but all together the student population was too large for one high school.

The grade school had a new teacher for the sixth grade. He was the younger brother of my former sixth grade teacher. His name was David Thompson, and he went to the Southern Methodist church and sometimes loafed with us at Rips in the evening. This was his first job, I was sure.

Well... he asked me for a date to a basketball game! I was stunned. I'd never had a date with anybody that old! I was flattered and excited and answered yes. What I didn't know until later was that he had asked Mother if she minded, and since she knew and liked his family, she had told him that it was fine with her.

I didn't want to wear just anything; after all, he was an "older man." I was accustomed to wearing a sweater and skirt and penny loafers with matching socks. I couldn't possibly wear that.

Mother had an outfit that I just adored; it would be a little large, but maybe we could fix it some way. It was a long leopard jacket with a green wool dress and a leopard "skull cap" and muff. She had bought it at Jenny's in Cincinnati. I asked her if I could wear it, and not wanting to burst my bubble, she said yes. I couldn't wear the dress, but I had a green wool skirt and a beige turtleneck sweater that would do. And, of course, I would wear heels and hose.

David came by for me at seven o'clock. I met him at the door in my sweater and skirt and skull cap and took him into the music room where Mother was reading. They had a short conversation while I went to get my coat, I mean Mother's coat, and muff. He held my coat for me and told me how nice I looked. I had not told any of my friends that I had a date with David or that I was wearing Mother's clothes, so they were more than a little surprised to see us together.

After the game we went to Rips to get a snack. We sat alone in a booth and had grilled cheese sandwiches and Cokes (he had coffee). All my friends came in and spoke to us, but nobody sat down with us. David was good company and had a keen sense of humor. I had a really nice evening and enjoyed David, but I didn't think I would wear heels and hose and a fur jacket to a basketball game again.

XXVII.

THE TIME HAD COME

It was my senior year, and in May I would graduate. It had been a fast four years. But there were still things left to do before May, like the senior play, "Don't Take My Penny." After the auditions I won the role of Penny. My friend David Whites from across the street was to play opposite me. The rehearsals would be such fun since we were all old friends. We practiced on Monday, Wednesday and Friday nights at the high school auditorium, I had been in the junior play, too. I had played the maid and borrowed Mattie's white apron and cap and worn a black dress.

We had six weeks of practice before the play opened. It would play on consecutive nights, Friday and Saturday. We sold lots of tickets;

the auditorium would be almost full. Of course, all our families would come to support us, as would our classmates and other students. We worked and practiced hard on the play, and it was a big success. We used the money we made from the ticket sales to buy new slipcovers for the stage furniture.

I was also editor of *The Scarlack*, our high school annual. It had to be ready by graduation, so we had a lot to do. It was a good group of friends; we had fun working together.

After Christmas our principal, Mr. Boyd, called me to his office. I wondered why and was a little apprehensive, but I knew I hadn't done anything wrong. When I got there his secretary told me to go on in.

Mr. Boyd stood up and motioned me to the chair in front of his desk. He said "Sydney Burns, have you been keeping track of your grades throughout high school?"

I replied, "No, sir, I just know that I've always tried to be on the Honor Roll."

"Well," he continued, "you've done a little better than that. You're the class valedictorian."

"I am?" I said with surprise.

"Yes, you are, and by telling you now I hope you will have enough time to prepare your valedictory address."

I knew my grades had been good, but I

didn't know they had been THAT good! I could hardly wait to get home and tell Mother! Then the next thing I would do was write Margaret.

My thoughts quickly returned to my valedictory address; I had momentarily forgotten that valedictorians had to make a speech. I couldn't DO that. What would I say? By the time I got home I was more worried about having to make a speech than I was pleased about being the valedictorian.

I told Mother and immediately said that I couldn't possibly give the valedictory address. She said, "I'm so proud of you! We'll talk about your address later. I'll call Shirley and Aunt Lill." My family and friends were pleased (including Margaret), but that didn't help my anxiety over the speech.

Mother said that your mind was always freshest in the morning, so she began getting me up an hour earlier before breakfast so I could work on the speech. In the meantime I had to prepare for the state achievement tests given to all Kentucky seniors to see how well the high schools compared. I could hardly afford to be the valedictorian and then turn around and do poorly on the achievement tests.

It was getting to be "crunch time." I worked on the speech every morning. I had decided that I should get three pieces of white paper that would fit in the palm of my hand, and on each piece I would write the first words or a line of the speech—not so much that I would find it hard to read on the stage, just enough to keep me on track. I numbered each line so I wouldn't get mixed up. I made only three lines to a page, so that wasn't so bad. I practiced with the slips of paper in my palm until it felt easy and the words came naturally.

I couldn't help thinking, though, "How did I get myself into this situation?" As I had said years before, "Who wants to go to college anyway!" Only THIS time Margaret hadn't found fault with my English. I had done this to myself.

The results from our state tests came back, and would wonders never cease—I had scored in the upper 5 percent of all the seniors in Kentucky in English! (This from the girl who couldn't pronounce "lingerie"!)

I was thrilled by the results. Then I was surprised by another coveted award, I was given the 6th annual award of *The Reader's Digest* Association "in recognition of past accomplishments and in anticipation of unusual achievements to come." I was to receive an honorary year's subscription to *The Reader's Digest* and an engraved certificate from the editors. Mr. Boyd and the teaching staff had submitted my name to *The Reader's Digest*.

The baccalaureate service was held on Sunday evening at the high school auditorium.

We wore our caps and gowns, and the minister from the Northern Methodist church, Rev. Seevers, spoke to us. The Southern Methodist church organist, Mrs. Armstrong, played for the service.

Graduation Day had arrived. It was May 11th and sunny and warm. We had been in summer clothes for the last two weeks. Tonight we would really get hot wearing our caps and gowns. The graduation exercises were to begin at 8 p.m., and we were all at the auditorium in plenty of time.

At exactly 8 p.m. the class began to walk down the aisle to the strains of "Pomp and Circumstance." That song always gave me an excited feeling; it had such a well-defined tempo. However, tonight I was REALLY excited! I didn't get to march in with my classmates; I came in earlier from backstage with our super-intendent, Mr. Cheek; our principal, Mr. Boyd; our commencement speaker, President W.F. O'Donnell of Eastern Kentucky State College; salutatorian Authena Cooper; and Reverend J. C. Hager of the Baptist church.

Reverend Hager gave the invocation, and then the salutatorian gave her address. Now it was my turn. I walked to the edge of the stage and looked out at my classmates; Bobby and David were sitting on the front row, and instead of looking up at me they were looking at the floor. They didn't want to catch my eye. This was not a funny time like we usually had, and they wanted to help me. I recognized all the dignitaries on stage, and then I began the speech.

The first thing on my agenda was recognizing a member of our class. Phillip Skaggs had been with us from the first grade, but last year he had volunteered for the Marines, even though he was underage, and earlier this year he had been killed in action. This brought a somber and sad note to our graduation.

The Second World War had been going on while we were in high school, but it hadn't changed our lives because none of the boys in my class was old enough to go to the war. My stepfather, Mr. Vinson (who was now Major Vinson), had been in the Air Force and in England for three years. I know that Mother was very lonesome, even though they wrote to each other every day. I had knitted a scarf for him.

I finished the speech before I knew it. It had gone faster and better than I had expected. I hadn't forgotten a word! The class filed across the stage and received their diplomas from Superintendent Cheek, and all of a sudden it was over. High school and the last four years of our lives were now history.

Mother had already sent out invitations to a porch dance at our house in two weeks. The porch was perfect; with the furniture removed it made a large dance floor. The weather would be ideal, not too hot. Mother had long pads made for the stone wall surrounding the porch (we didn't have flowers there anymore), and there would also be chairs on the patio where we could sit. But best of all, my cousins Rachael and Eula Carroll would be there, and Mary Jane was coming back for a visit, too. The immediate future looked bright.

Louisa High School

XVIII.

THE END

I had mixed feelings about going off to college in the fall. I would miss my friends, sledding on the town hill, ice skating on the Big Sandy, all those football and basketball games, and riding in that old Model A Ford that I helped to paint. I would even miss playing the old pump organ on Sunday nights at our M.Y.F. meetings. It would indeed be hard for me to leave my family and this place I loved so well, I suppose this was all part of "growing up," and already the next group of seniors had begun taking our places. But the things I was taking with me would endure forever—my faith in God, the love of my family, and my sense of humor.

You have met the people I loved and traveled the years that were, so until next time—God bless.